MY BODY
MY BODY H
EYES

AMY CULLIFORD

A Crabtree Roots Plus Book

CRABTREE
Publishing Company
www.crabtreebooks.com

School-to-Home Support for Caregivers and Teachers

This book helps children grow by letting them practice reading. Here are a few guiding questions to help the reader with building his or her comprehension skills. Possible answers appear here in red.

Before Reading:

• What do I think this book is about?
- *I think this book is about my eyes.*
- *I think this book is about how my eyes work.*

• What do I want to learn about this topic?
- *I want to learn why people have different colored eyes.*
- *I want to learn how my eyes can see.*

During Reading:

• I wonder why...
- *I wonder why I only have two eyes.*
- *I wonder why some people need glasses.*

• What have I learned so far?
- *I have learned that my eyes need light to see.*
- *I have learned that my eyes can see both near and far.*

After Reading:

• What details did I learn about this topic?
- *I have learned that some people cannot see. They are blind.*
- *I have learned that a flashlight can help me see in the dark.*

• Read the book again and look for the vocabulary words.
- *I see the word **shapes** on page 10 and the word **blind** on page 17. The other vocabulary words are found on page 23.*

You have two **eyes**.

They are on your **face**.

What **color** are your eyes?

Look over there!

What do you see?

I see my school!

Your eyes help you see things. Your eyes can see **shapes**!

Eyes can see things
that are near.

Eyes can see things that are far.

Some people need
help to see clearly.
They wear **glasses**.

You can see things
when there is light.

You can use a **flashlight**
to see when it is dark!

Some people cannot see at all. They are **blind**.

Eyes help you read words and numbers.

Your eyes help you
read this book!

Word List

Sight Words

a	light	there
all	look	they
and	my	things
are	near	this
at	need	to
book	numbers	two
can	on	use
do	over	wear
eyes	people	what
far	read	when
have	school	words
help	see	you
I	some	your
is	that	

Words to Know

blind

color

eyes

face

flashlight glasses shapes

MY BODY
MY BODY HAS
EYES

Written by: Amy Culliford

Designed by: Rhea Wallace

Series Development: James Earley

Proofreader: Janine Deschenes

Educational Consultant: Marie Lemke M.Ed.

Print and production coordinator:

Katherine Berti

Photographs:
Shutterstock: New Africa: cover, p. 3, 5; Tetyana Kaganska: p. 4; Amir Bajric: p. 7; Cynthia Farmer: p.9; Ivonne Wrerink: p. 11; Elena Masiutkina: p. 12; Maples images: p. 13; Seventy Four: p. 14, 23; Svitlanch Bezuhlova: p. 15; Yuganov Konstantin: p. 16; Andrey_Popov: p. 17; Shchus: p. 19; POP-THAILAND: p. 21

Library and Archives Canada Cataloguing in Publication

Available at the Library and Archives Canada

Library of Congress Cataloging-in-Publication Data

Available at the Library of Congress

Crabtree Publishing Company

Printed in the U.S.A./CG20210915/012022

www.crabtreebooks.com   1-800-387-7650

Published in the United States
Crabtree Publishing
347 Fifth Avenue, Suite 1402-145
New York, NY, 10016

Published in Canada
Crabtree Publishing
616 Welland Ave.
St. Catharines, Ontario L2M 5V6